CONSERVATIONISTS

WILL STEGER

JOANNE MATTERN

ABDO Publishing Company

visit us at
www.abdopublishing.com

Published by ABDO Publishing Company, PO Box 398166, Minneapolis, MN 55439.
Copyright © 2014 by Abdo Consulting Group, Inc. International copyrights reserved in all
countries. No part of this book may be reproduced in any form without written permission from the
publisher. The Checkerboard Library™ is a trademark and logo of ABDO Publishing Company.

Printed in the United States of America, North Mankato, Minnesota.
112013
012014

 PRINTED ON RECYCLED PAPER

Cover Photos: AP Images; iStockphoto
Interior Photos: AP Images pp. 25, 27; BRUCE DALE/National Geographic Creative p. 7; Corbis
  pp. 5, 13; Getty Images pp. 18–19, 21; GORDON WILTSIE/National Geographic Creative
  pp. 17, 20; iStockphoto p. 1; JIM BRANDENBURG/National Geographic Creative pp. 8, 23;
  KENT KOBERSTEEN/National Geographic Creative p. 11; Superstock p. 15

Editors: Rochelle Baltzer, Tamara L. Britton, Bridget O'Brien
Art Direction: Neil Klinepier

Library of Congress Cataloging-in-Publication Data

Mattern, Joanne.
  Will Steger / Joanne Mattern.
     p. cm. -- (Conservationists)
  Includes index.
  ISBN 978-1-62403-096-3
1. Steger, Will--Juvenile literature. 2. Explorers--United States--Biography--Juvenile literature.
3. Arctic regions--Discovery and exploration--American--Juvenile literature. 4. North Pole--
Discovery and exploration--American--Juvenile literature. I. Title.
  G630.A5S7335 2014
  910.911'3--dc23
                              2013035923

CONTENTS

A Spirit of Adventure

Will Steger has experienced Earth's most extreme **environments**. In his travels, he has seen firsthand the effects of **global warming** in the Arctic and Antarctic. Today, he educates others about this serious threat.

Will was born in Mahtomedi, Minnesota, on August 27, 1944. He was the second of Bill and Margaret Steger's nine children. Will's parents encouraged their children to pursue their own interests. As a young man, Will developed a spirit of adventure.

Will's interest in science began early. When he was 12 years old, he took part in a science education project called the 1957–58 International Geophysical Year. Students worldwide made observations and conducted experiments.

Will observed the night sky from his Minnesota home and mapped the **aurora borealis**.

Three years later, Will and his brother Tom traveled down the Mississippi River in a motorboat. Their journey took them all the way to New Orleans, Louisiana.

Will enjoyed the trip, but he didn't like traveling by motorboat. He decided that trip would be his first and last motorized adventure. But that didn't mean he planned to stay home.

Will Steger is the first person to reach both the North and South Poles by dogsled.

INTO THE WILDERNESS

In 1962, Steger hitchhiked alone to Alaska. He kayaked the Yukon River. Two years later, he kayaked 3,000 miles (4,828 km) from Alberta, Canada, to Alaska. In following years, Steger traveled through the Alaskan and Canadian wilderness several times. Then in 1965, he climbed two mountains in Peru that were 19,000 feet (5,791 m) high!

In his adventures, Will did not neglect his education. In 1966, he earned a degree in **geology** from the University of St. Thomas in St. Paul, Minnesota. After graduation, Steger became a science teacher. However, his heart was in the wilderness. He thought about how he could combine teaching with outdoor adventure.

In 1969, Steger earned a graduate degree in education from St. Thomas. He took time off from his work to take a

Many of Steger's adventures have started from the Homestead's backyard.

4,000-mile (6,437-km) kayak trip on the Mackenzie, Peace, and Yukon Rivers in Canada and Alaska.

In 1970, Steger moved to Ely, Minnesota. There, he built a small cabin in the woods. He called it the Homestead. The cabin had no electricity or running water. Steger grew most of his own food. He lived a lifestyle that did not harm the earth.

To earn money, Steger led canoe trips and taught at an **Outward Bound** school. In 1973, he started his own school. He called it the Lynx Track Winter Skills School.

MEETING THE CHALLENGE

Some days, the sleds traveled quickly over the snow. Other days, Steger and his team had to chop through walls of ice. Sometimes they helped the dogs by pushing the sleds through deep snow. Other times they used **peaveys** to pry stuck sleds from the snow.

North to the Pole
Will Steger
Paul Schurke
Ann Bancroft
Brent Boddy
Geoff Carroll
Bob Mantell
Bob McKerrow
Richard Weber

This was dangerous work. On April 2, Bob McKerrow was hit by a sled. He suffered several broken ribs. The injury forced him to leave the team.

The team faced bitter cold. Several members had frozen fingers and toes. Their skin froze and their eyes froze shut. **Frostbite** on Bob Mantell's feet became so bad he also had to leave the team.

Steger and his teammates pushed on through the extreme conditions. Finally, on May 1, the team reached the North Pole. They had done it! It was the first confirmed journey on dogsleds without resupply from the outside.

The six team members who arrived at the North Pole included Ann Bancroft (third from left), *the first woman to reach the pole on foot.*

THE NEXT ADVENTURE

While on the North Pole trip, Steger met Frenchman Jean-Louis Etienne. Etienne was skiing to the North Pole. Steger and Etienne visited for a while. They discovered both wanted to travel to Antarctica. They made plans to meet later and discuss the trip.

Steger had important plans for an Antarctic trip. **Global warming** and pollution were harming plant and animal life there. Steger wanted to educate people about the hole in the earth's **ozone layer** and other dangers to the Antarctic **environment**. In addition, the 1959 Antarctic Treaty was about to expire. Steger wanted to show that the treaty should be renewed.

The 1959 Antarctic Treaty preserved Antarctica as a research station and encouraged free scientific exchange between nations. It also banned nuclear testing there. The treaty was renewed on October 4, 1991, with a fifty-year ban on mining.

To prepare for the trip, Steger and Etienne decided to travel across Greenland. They would consider which teammates to include on the trip to Antarctica.

In 1988, they spent 62 days traveling 1,600 miles (2,575 km) from south to north across the Greenland ice cap. They learned about each other and became friends. At the time, it was the longest unsupported dogsled expedition in history.

Jean-Louis Etienne became the first person to reach the North Pole on skis.

THE SOUTH POLE

Once again, Steger had to raise money to pay for the expedition. He raised $10 million. Finally, on July 27, 1989, Steger, Etienne, and four other men began the International Trans-Antarctica Expedition.

International Trans-Antarctica Expedition
Will Steger – United States
Jean-Louis Etienne – France
Victor Boyarsky – Russia
Qin Dahe – China
Keizo Funatsu – Japan
Geoff Somers – United Kingdom

On this trip, the team would receive new supplies along the way. Before the trip began, **caches** had been dropped by airplanes along the route. Airplanes would also drop off supplies during the trip.

Like the Arctic, the Antarctic **environment** was cold and icy. But during this journey, the weather was much worse.

In September, the team was hit by winds that blew at 100 miles per hour (161 km/h). The storm lasted for 11 days. During the storm, Steger and his teammates huddled in their tents. After the storm ended, they were able to move on.

Steger walks among Adélie penguins. Their population has decreased as sea ice has melted.

STEGER'S ANTARCTIC ADVENTURES

Many more storms hit during the next few weeks. The cold was hard on the men and the dogs. **Frostbitten** skin and cracked fingers made everyday tasks difficult and painful. The extreme cold kept the dogs from getting enough sleep.

On December 11, the team arrived at the United States' Amundsen/Scott South Pole Station. It had taken 137 days to travel 2,000 miles (3,219 km).

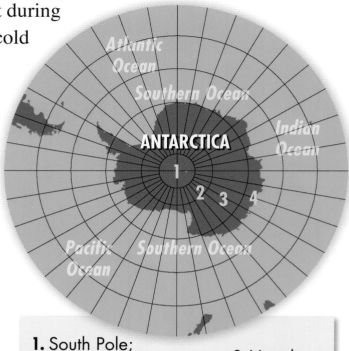

1. South Pole; Amundsen/ Scott South Pole Station
2. Area of Inaccessibility
3. Vostok
4. Mirnyy

The next stop was the Soviet Union station Vostok, 1,200 miles (1,931 km) away.

To get there, Steger and his team had to travel through the **area of inaccessibility**. This 800-mile (1,287-km) area had

Sled dogs sleep outside. Snow buries them and insulates them from the cold.

never before been crossed on foot. They had to travel quickly. If they did not complete their journey by March, they would be trapped in Antarctica through the long winter.

The team reached Vostok on January 18, 1990. They were three-quarters of the way across Antarctica. After a rest, Steger and his team headed out once more. In the middle of February, they saw seabirds flying overhead. This meant they were near Antarctica's coast and the end of their journey.

SUCCESS

By March 1, Steger and the team were less than 100 miles (161 km) away from the Soviet base Mirnyy. Then, a terrible blizzard hit. Once again, they had to stop.

That night, Keizo Funatsu left his tent. He became lost in the blizzard. The team searched for him until it was too dark to see.

The next morning, they quickly restarted the search. Amazingly, they found Funatsu alive. He had spent the night in a snow trench he had dug with a pair of pliers.

With Funatsu safe, the team moved on. On March 3, the team rode into Mirnyy. Many people were there to greet

them. Their arrival was broadcast on French television. It had taken seven months for Steger and his team to travel 3,741 miles (6,021 km) across Antarctica. It was the first dogsled crossing of Antarctica.

FUN FACT:
Around the world, 15 million students followed the expedition in their classrooms.

THE ARCTIC PROJECT

Steger on the Arctic Ocean

In 1992, Steger began training for another trip across the Arctic Ocean. For the next two years, Will and his teammates traveled throughout Canada to practice for their trip. Will helped develop layered, warm clothing and sleeping bags to keep the explorers warm.

In 1995, Steger led the International Arctic Project. The team would travel 2,500 miles (4,023 km) from Russia's Cape Arkticheskiy in Siberia across the North Pole to Canada's Ward Hunt Island.

From left to right: *Takano, Boyarsky, Vedel, Steger, Hanson, and Hignell, with Steger's former wife Patti Holmberg* (center)

For the first part of the journey, the team would travel by dogsled. Later, they would send the dogs home in airplanes. Then, the team would travel by canoe-sled.

The expedition got off to a shaky start. The ice shifted a lot. A team of dogs went into the water. While trying to save them, Ulrik Vedel fell in too. The team had to return to its starting point. A helicopter later flew them to a starting point past the unstable ice. But Vedel chose not to remain with the team.

International Arctic Project
Will Steger – United States
Ulrik Vedel – Denmark
Victor Boyarsky – Russia
Takako Takano – Japan
Julie Hanson – United States
Martin Hignell – United Kingdom

ARCTIC IN PERIL

The International Arctic Project was more than just a journey. The Arctic was becoming polluted. Contaminants were being carried up from the south by wind and water currents. Warming temperatures were affecting the temperature of the oceans and changing weather patterns.

Steger wanted to teach children about this and inspire them to protect the **environment**. During the journey, Steger and his team used the Internet to share journal entries and photographs with schoolchildren all over the world. About 25 million students followed the expedition on their computers.

In June, warm temperatures resulted in melting ice. The dogs were flown out on June 16. The 20-foot (6-m) long canoe-sleds moved easily over water. But they had to be pulled through the snow.

CONSERVATION ALERT!

If current warming continues, lost sea ice will result in the loss of two-thirds of the polar bear population by 2050.

*Sled dogs traveling in
an airplane*

On July 3, after 116 days on the ice, the team reached land. It was the first time anyone had traveled across the surface of the Arctic Ocean in one season.

SAVING EARTH

Steger started the Will Steger Foundation in 2006. Its goal is to educate people about the effects of **climate change**. It encourages them to work together to develop solutions through education and public policy. Steger wants to save wild places and protect the **environment**.

In addition to his foundation, Steger also reaches people through his writing. He has written four books for children and adults. These books are *Over the Top of the World*, *Crossing Antarctica*, *North to the Pole*, and *Saving the Earth*.

In 2013, Steger created the Steger Wilderness Center for Innovation and Leadership at the Homestead. There, people can meet to develop solutions to environmental challenges.

In recognition of his work, Steger has won many awards. These include the National Geographic Society's John Oliver La Gorce Medal in 1995.

Will Steger has been to some of the most dangerous and extreme places on our planet. Through his explorations and his work, he has shown people around the world that every place on Earth is worth saving. Today, he continues working to keep Earth sustainable for future generations.

TIMELINE

1944 Will Steger was born in Mahtomedi, Minnesota, on August 27.

1957 Steger participated in the International Geophysical Year.

1966 Steger graduated from the University of St. Thomas with a degree in geology. Three years later he received a graduate degree in education.

1970 Steger moved to Ely, Minnesota, and built the Homestead.

1973 Steger started the Lynx Track Winter Skills School.

1986 The Steger International Polar Expedition completed the first trip to the North Pole without resupply.

1988 Steger led an international team on the first trip from south to north across the Greenland ice cap, the longest unsupported dogsled expedition in history.

1990 The International Trans-Antarctica Expedition completed the first crossing of Antarctica by dogsled.

1995 The International Arctic Project completed the first crossing of the Arctic Ocean in one season.

2004 ● The Arctic Transect Expedition traveled across Nunavut Territory in Canada and collected information about global warming issues.

2006 ● Steger formed the Will Steger Foundation to educate people about the environment.

2007 ● The Global Warming 101 Expedition traveled across Canada's Baffin Island and studied the effects of global warming on native peoples.

2013 ● Steger created the Steger Wilderness Center for Innovation and Leadership at the Homestead.

"The Arctic is both my teacher and my classroom."

—Will Steger

GLOSSARY

area of inaccessibility - the point on the Antarctic continent farthest from the Southern Ocean.

aurora borealis - light in the sky in Earth's northern hemisphere caused by atoms moving along the planet's magnetic field.

cache - a secure or hidden place in which to store something. Something stored in such a place can also be called a cache.

carbon dioxide - a heavy, colorless gas that is formed when fuel containing the element carbon is burned.

climate change - a long-term change in Earth's climate, or in that of a region of Earth. It includes changing temperatures, weather patterns, and more. It can result from natural processes or human activities.

environment - all the surroundings that affect the growth and well-being of a living thing.

fossil fuel - a fuel formed in the earth from the remains of plants or animals. Coal, oil, and natural gas are fossil fuels.

frostbite - the freezing of the tissues of a body part, such as a hand.

geology - the science of Earth and its structure. A person who studies geology is called a geologist.

global warming - an increase in the temperature of Earth's atmosphere and oceans.

indigenous - native to a certain place.

Outward Bound - an educational program in which students gain self-esteem and learn responsibility to others through hands-on learning in outdoor adventures.

ozone layer - a layer 20 to 30 miles (32 to 48 km) above Earth's surface. It blocks ultraviolet radiation from coming into the lower atmosphere.

peavey - a pole with a metal spike on the end.

WEB SITES

To learn more about Will Steger, visit ABDO Publishing Company online. Web sites about Will Steger are featured on our Book Links page. These links are routinely monitored and updated to provide the most current information available.
www.abdopublishing.com

INDEX